Decorative Painting

*Techniques and Designs
for Transforming Everyday Objects*

Tahira Lewis

HAND BOOKS PRESS

MADISON, WISCONSIN

DISTRIBUTED BY NORTH LIGHT BOOKS

CINCINNATI, OHIO

First published in the U.S.A. by Hand Books Press
931 East Main Street #106
Madison, WI 53703–2955 U.S.A.

ISBN 0-9658248-2-9

02 01 00 99 98 5 4 3 2 1

Distributed to the book trade and art trade in the U.S.A. by
North Light Books, an imprint of F&W Publications
1507 Dana Avenue, Cincinnati, Ohio 45207
Telephone: (800) 289-0963, Fax: (513) 531-4082

DEDICATION
To Stephen, Jason and Natasha, my wonderful family, for all their sacrifices.

ACKNOWLEDGEMENTS
I wish to thank all my friends, teachers and students for their help and
encouragement. With very special thanks to Phillip Chambers, Ann
Whitchell, Karen Gunnell and Farnosh Zahab for lightening the load,
and to Venetia Penfold for all her help and guidance. I couldn't have had
a better editor to tackle the difficult task of turning a painter into a writer.

Cover design by Stephen Bridges
Photography by Marie-Louise Avery
except page 68 which is by Shona Wood

Printed and bound in China

Contents

Introduction

Change your life and pick up a brush and paint!

In this book, I would like to show those of you who think freehand painting is the prerogative of the chosen few how, with simple techniques, you can transform everyday items in your own home and create tomorrow's heirlooms.

Everyone is creative. All too often as children you were made to feel that you either had the 'gift' or you didn't. There is no doubt that some people are especially gifted artistically, just as some people are great writers or mathematicians. However, this doesn't mean that we should not be taught how to hold a pen, form letters, build words and compose sentences. That is exactly what learning decorative painting is all about; how to hold a brush, mix colour, load a brush, form the basic strokes and create designs. These are all techniques which can be learned.

Can't draw? I couldn't draw when I first started. All you really need is the ability to trace and after a few patterns you too will find that you are learning how to draw.

Don't be discouraged with your first attempts; just keep practising and in a surprisingly short time you will get there. Correcting mistakes is all part of discovering how to be creative and daring again. If you make mistakes, so what? Nothing is carved in stone. You can always sand it off, paint over it again or, like me, just hide it at the back of the garage until you are ready to face it again!

Remember that everyone's handwriting is different – so your painting will have its own unique style. Sometimes my students bemoan the fact that their work doesn't look like mine, but it would be a shame if it did, because it is good to let your own character and sense of colour express itself in your painting. It is exciting to see a range of styles and I am constantly delighted by my students' individual and original use of colour and technique. Don't take yourself or your painting too seriously; in Somerset Maugham's words,

Perfection has one big defect. It is apt to be dull.

The fact that decorative and folk art painting does not concern itself with realism allows for a wonderful spontaneity of expression. *Spontaneity* – remember that word every time you pick up a brush.

Once you have mastered the basics you will be able to refine the various techniques and projects shown in this book and take your painting to whatever level suits you.

The history of decorative art

The art of decorating your home environment is a tradition which dates back to prehistoric man. All cultures seem to have a deep need to enhance their surroundings and the decorative styles and range of artefacts produced throughout the history of mankind continue to influence our everyday life.

Painted furniture as we know it today has its roots in the seventeenth century. As trade with the Far East developed, the fashion for oriental painted furniture grew rapidly amongst the monarchy and aristocracy of Europe. The long process of creating lacquerware in China and Japan plus the protracted shipping times meant that orders often took years to complete. European cabinet makers, looking for ways to emulate these products in response to popular demand, created a style called Chinoiserie. The decorative painters in the eighteenth and nineteenth centuries added new styles and techniques to this fashion to meet the demands of their customers. This included the development of designs which interpreted the decorative styles of the Middle Ages and Renaissance.

In Northern and Eastern Europe, the demand for painted furniture filtered down from the aristocracy to the lower levels of society and was interpreted according to the population's means and needs. Perhaps it was due to the long hard winters that the tradition of women decorating their own household furnishings developed.

Folk Art in England developed along rather different lines and was mainly enjoyed by the aristocracy. In the eighteenth century, the architect, Robert Adam, inspired by the Italian example, designed furniture which was then decorated by professional artists such as Angelica Kauffmann in a style which reflected the architectural setting. Tole and pâpier maché of this period was mostly decorated in the factories where they were produced.

Travelling showmen were the first to decorate caravans in the eighteenth century, rather than the gypsies who didn't take to the roads until the late eighteenth century. The particular style of castles and roses used on the canal boats was probably brought to England by the Romany gypsies; the castles depicting the typically Eastern European onion-top roofs. The barges only started to be decorated as this method of transport went into decline. Consequently, the family was conscripted to supply cheap or free labour and as a result, the barges became their homes – hence the need for decoration.

Early American colonists in the seventeenth century were influenced by the decorative traditions of migrating Europeans. A new impetus for decorative painting came in the mid-eighteenth century when religious upheavals in Europe sent a flood of migrants to the new world from Germany, Holland, Switzerland, Silesia and Moravia. Many settled in Pennsylvania. The women took on this art form as part of their homemaking skills, infusing it with a wonderful vitality as they decorated virtually every object in the home. It is interesting to note that a trade which was predominately the domain of men has been left to women to revive.

Chapter 1

MATERIALS
AND
TECHNIQUES

In this chapter you will learn how to master the practical skills required for the 20 stunning projects which follow. After a comprehensive list of materials, an illustrated step-by-step guide shows how to perform the variety of brushstrokes used throughout the book. In addition, there is a section on techniques for preparing surfaces plus different methods for creating a variety of backgrounds.

Materials

The huge range and high standard of paints, brushes and other materials available will give you the flexibility to create the exciting effects shown in this book.

PAINT

This book focuses on the use of acrylic paint as the most popular choice for decorative art. Acrylic paint is non-inflammable, non-toxic and flows easily while allowing the controlled application of the paint. It is not necessary to buy a great range of colours to get started.

I would recommend the following colour range for beginners: Yellow Oxide, Burnt Umber, Hooker's Green, Alizarin Crimson, Cobalt Blue, Titanium White, Antique White and Black. In order to broaden the range of colours available, you could add colours with basic pigments such as Cadmium Yellow, Cadmium Orange, Purple Dioxide and Turquoise. Ready-mixed colours also have their place, offering the convenience of having your favourite colours to hand.

I use my own brand of Tahira's Acrylic Paint but other brands available are Liquitex, Folk Art, Deco Art, Jo Sonja and Matisse. Most of the colours used for the projects in this book can be made up from half a dozen pure pigment colours. Traditional artists' colours form part of an international colour classification and are available with oil, watercolour or acrylic paints.

BRUSHES

There are different types of brushes suitable for decorative painting. Brushes made from Taklon are popular, inexpensive and easily available.

There are a large variety of brush shapes which have been specially designed to enable you to achieve effective strokes with ease. I would advise you to start with the two standard shapes, a No. 4 round brush and a No. 6 flat brush. Each project gives individual details of the range of brushes required, so don't buy them until you have decided which projects to tackle. You can extend your range of brushes as your technique develops.

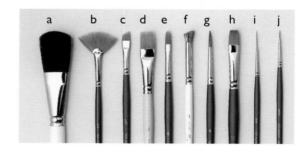

Round brush (No. 1, 2, 4, 6)

The ferrule of the round brush is cylindrical and this gives the brush its name (Fig. g on photograph). The hairs of the brush are shorter on the outer edges, increasing in length towards the centre so the brush head comes to a fine point. This is the traditional brush for stroke work but it can also be used for shading and blending.

Flat brush (No. 4, 6, 8, 12, 18)

Also called a shader brush, this has a flattened ferrule with the hairs cut straight across the top which is referred to as the chisel edge (Fig. h). These brushes are particularly good for shading and highlighting but are also used for stroke work. An angle shader is the same as a flat brush but the chisel edge is cut at an angle (Fig. c).

Deer foot stippler (No. 4, 6)

These are round brushes made with stiff hairs with the head cut at an angle (Fig. f). They are ideal for creating foliage or fur.

Glazing mop

These are round brushes with large, rounded heads like a make-up brush, also known as softening brushes (Fig. a). They are used on open paintwork to soften lines when antiquing or marbling. They should be used with retarder for acrylic paint and must be washed immediately after use.

Liner brush (No. 5/0)

Liner brushes are thin, round brushes with long hairs which act as an ink well for watered down paint, allowing you to pull long lines and swirls (Fig. i). They are ideal for outlining and veining.

Detail brush (No. 10/0)

This round brush has just a few short, fine hairs and is used for fine, detailed work (Fig. j).

Comb/Fan brush (1 cm/½ in.)

Also called a rake brush, this brush is thinned at the tip in a flat or fan shape. It is useful for painting grass, hair, fur and wood grain effects (Fig. d and Fig. b for comb and fan brush respectively).

Filbert brush (No. 6)

The filbert brush is the same as a flat brush, but the corners of the chisel end are rounded off, making the end an oval shape (Fig. e). When used for shading and blending they give a softer edge and are handy for creating quick petals and leaves.

Sponge brush (2 cm/1 in., 4 cm/1½ in., 7 cm/2¾ in.)

Also called a foam brush, this brush is a wedge of sponge with a little stiffening in the centre. It is used for background painting and reaches awkward corners. Make sure it is slightly dampened before use and squeeze the excess water out on an old towel.

Varnishing brush (4 cm/1½ in.)

This is a wide, flat Taklon brush with fine hairs to give a smooth finish. It is a worthwhile investment as finishing needs as much care as decoration.

Brush care

When using a dry brush, always soak it first thoroughly in water and wipe off excess on a tissue. Rinse your brushes regularly and make sure that you keep them immersed in water until you have time to clean them. Do not allow paint to build up in the ferrule while you are painting as this will make it difficult to produce good strokes. Brushes should not be left standing in jars of water as this will quickly damage the tip. Brush basins have the advantage of keeping the bristles immersed in the water while preventing the tip of the brush touching the bottom of the jar. When painting, treat your brush gently and do not scrub it round and round on the palette.

When you have finished painting, wash your brushes out in cold water with a little soap. Gently work the bristles around to make sure all the paint has come out of the ferrule. If paint is allowed to dry on the brush, it is hard to remove without damaging the bristles. After you have finished washing the brush, dab it on a tissue. If colour is still coming out then wash it again.

EQUIPMENT

A list of basic equipment is outlined below. Each project provides a list of materials, so don't buy everything until you see what you need.

Art carbon

Also called transfer paper, this wax-free, chalk-backed, carbon paper is used with tracing paper for transferring designs. It is available in various colours, so choose the colours according to the paints you are using so that the carbon colour does not show through. Do not use ordinary carbon paper, as the colour will bleed into the paintwork. Sometimes the art carbon marks can be a little stubborn to erase, in which case a tissue dampened with a little white spirit will quickly remove them without harming the paint.

Brown paper bags

Paper bags are excellent to use for smoothing edges and buffing surfaces.

Eraser

A good quality soft eraser is needed for removing any pattern lines left showing. This must be done before antiquing or varnishing.

Liquid masking

This is a rubber solution used as an adhesive in the carpet industry which has been repacked as liquid masking and is available through art shops. It is useful for masking off small surface areas. Apply with an old brush dampened with water and rinse it immediately. When applied to a smooth painted surface and left to dry it can be peeled off by rubbing with your finger.

Low tack tape

Low tack sticky tape is an alternative way of masking off an area while painting another. It is ideal for masking off large areas and creating straight lines.

Paint roller

A small sponge roller enables the easy application of background paint and varnish to large items. They give a slightly textured, even background.

Palette knife

This is useful for mixing larger quantities of paint rather than using your brush.

Palette

Acrylic paints dry permanently, so once left to dry, cannot be reused. Waxed paper or an old tile can be used or a wet palette which allows you to use the paint for longer. To make your own wet palette, wet a jaycloth, squeeze it out gently and wrap a sheet of greaseproof paper around it. Then lay it flat on a tile or in a shallow food container. The paint palette can be kept moist in an airtight box for quite a few days.

PVA glue

This is a water-soluble, plastic-based glue used for a variety of purposes. In these projects it is used to key the surface before painting.

Retarder

Retarder, also known as extender, is used to slow down the drying of paint and increase its flow. For detailed work the retarder is used on the brush or rubbed into the area to be painted. Always use it sparingly. First load the brush with the retarder, take off the excess by resting the brush on a paper towel until the sheen disappears and then load the brush with the paint.

Sandpaper

Use a fine to medium fine, wet and dry

sandpaper. Sanding blocks are good for large areas and emery boards are ideal for small, awkward places.

Shellac, sanding sealer and white polish

These are three methods of sealing wood and french polishing. They all dry very quickly and prevent resins from seeping out of the knots of new timber. They are not water-based so use methylated spirit as a thinner and for cleaning brushes. I like to use them for sealing as they give an excellent finish. They are very tough on brushes so keep a special one aside.

Cocktail stick sponge

This is useful when finely stippling very small areas, for example the centre of flowers (see page 68). Fix a small piece of a very fine marine sponge on a cocktail stick. First break off the point of the stick, drape the sponge over the top and tie it with a piece of cotton. It should look slightly bigger than a cotton bud.

Marine sponge

The varying sizes and shapes make them ideal for creating different stippled paint effects.

Make-up sponges

These are good quality fine foam sponges which can be cut up and used for painting the edges, legs and spindles of chairs. One of these sponges dipped into the paint spreads the paint smoothly and quickly. Remember to use a small brush first to touch in around the joints and spindles.

Steel wool

000 steel wool is good for distressing painted items by removing a thin layer of paint without causing scratch marks.

Stylus

This is a pointed, metal tool with a fine, ball head. It can be used instead of a pen for tracing and avoids a build-up of lines on the tracing if it is used several times. It is also ideal for creating lace effects and dotting in stamens. Create lines or swirls of graduated dots by dipping the stylus into the paint and starting a line of dots which will diminish as the paint runs out. For the same size dots, pick up the paint as you progress.

Tack cloth

This is a tacky cloth for removing specks of dust before painting. (A damp sponge is also good.)

Tracing paper

Semi-transparent paper for transferring patterns.

Water-based varnish

Water-based varnishes can only be used over water-based paints unless the oil-based paint is very old. Most are ideal for mixing with acrylic paints to make clear, coloured glazes. Matt varnishes should be stirred well before use. Brushes should be washed out in soapy water.

Oil-based varnish

Oil-based varnishes can be applied over acrylics as well as oil-based paints. It is important to stir both satin and matt varnishes from the bottom to the top as the settling out is more pronounced than acrylic varnishes. Brushes need to be cleaned first in white spirit and then washed thoroughly with soap and water. Wash several times until the soap foams.

Do not load your brush straight from the pot for either type of varnish, as this will contaminate the varnish with dust and fibres. Pour what you need into a dish and discard the remainder. You can use high gloss, satin or matt varnish according to your preference.

Techniques

The techniques which follow are essential to the overall finish of your project. You will learn how to prepare a variety of surfaces, create a range of paint effects and experience the excitement of developing brushstroke and painting skills – once thought to be out of reach.

PREPARING SURFACES

It is essential to prepare the surfaces properly as they must be an effective base for painting and decoration. Grease, rust, dirt and fingermarks will all affect the overall finish. The quality and colour of the surface must be planned at this stage in relation to the finished piece.

Glass/Enamel

Glass surfaces can be painted with most acrylic paints but purely for decorative purposes. For example, acrylic may come off in the dishwasher. There are other specialized glass paints available which will give extra protection and can be used in the same way as acrylic. Prepare the surface for painting by washing and rinsing with a solution of 1-part vinegar to 2-parts water.

Metal

Careful preparation of metal surfaces is essential, as rust which is not properly treated will break through the paint. Rust should be removed with a wire brush or steel wool and the area cleaned with a solution of 1-part vinegar to 2-parts water. Dry the piece immediately and, if possible, place it in a slightly warm oven overnight to dry out any residual moisture which will restart the rust process. Rust-inhibiting paint, available from hardware stores, should be applied at this stage. You could also get a large, rusty piece sandblasted and primed.

Terracotta

Only use new terracotta pots, as used pots have accumulated salts which will affect the paint finish. Paint the inside and outside of the pot with a mix of 1-part PVA to 2-parts water until it saturates the surface. Then leave it to dry. It is now ready for painting.

MDF board

This consists of very fine wood fibres bonded with glue. Good quality MDF does not need sanding or sealing as it already has a surface preparation, so you will only need to sand the cut or routed edges. Sanding the finished surface will expose the fibres which will swell with the moisture from the paint and cause unnecessary work. On some MDF, water-based paints may cause fibres to swell. If this happens, buff the board with a crumpled brown paper bag or sand lightly with fine sandpaper between coats.

Wood

Natural wood grains can make effective backgrounds. Fill any holes or gaps with a wood filler that matches the colour of wood that you are using. Create a smooth surface with fine sandpaper or, if the surface is already smooth, buff with a brown paper bag. Always sand in the direction of the grain, paying special attention to the edges and joints.

Painted, wooden items can be stripped or sanded. If the item is in reasonable condition, the surface can be smoothed and cleaned for repainting. Use touch as well as sight to feel any bumps when you are sanding. Sand until smooth and wipe over the surface with white spirit to remove any dirt and grease. Use a tack cloth or a damp, lint-free cloth to remove any dust before moving to the next stage.

Sealing

It is not necessary to seal MDF board or wood before using acrylic water-based paints. If you want to paint using the wood grain as a background, paint your design directly on the wood. You could also use shellac or clear varnish to protect the surface (see page 11).

Wood staining

Staining allows the wood grain to show through the surface decoration. If possible, test a small area of the wood that is hidden from view.

First give it one or two coats of clear, watered-down varnish to seal the grain and any joints. This will prevent the stain from being absorbed unevenly. When dry, lightly sand with a fine grade paper or buff with a brown paper bag. It is not necessary to buy ready-prepared wood stains, especially if the project is small. Add a little acrylic paint of the colour you require with a little water to a water-based varnish (approximately 1-part water to 4-parts varnish). You now have a stain that can be applied to a finished surface or directly to the wood.

Painting the basecoat

When applying a background colour, always use a good quality brush. Wet your brush before dipping it in the paint and wipe off the excess water. Two or three thin coats of paint are preferable to using one thick layer which may create ridges of paint. Apply the paint with long,

even strokes. If you find the paint is drying before you have quite finished, pick up a little more water on the brush. When the first coat is dry, sand it lightly with fine sandpaper or buff with a paper bag. Make sure you always sand in the direction of the wood grain, then dust and repaint. When basecoating a large piece of MDF, I sometimes wipe it over with a damp cloth first. This stops the paint drying too quickly and gives it a very smooth finish. However, do not soak the MDF as it may make the fibres swell.

DESIGN

Once you have chosen your piece of furniture and prepared the surface, the next stage is to decide on the position of the design.

There are several methods to help you with layout and colour. You can lay the pattern on the item to be painted and stand back to see where you would like it to be positioned or trace and paint the design on a card painted in your chosen background colour. Alternatively the design can be painted on acetate or tracing paper, which you can lay on your project to see how it will look. You can also cut these up to rearrange the elements of the design.

Transferring a design

Firstly, trace the design. There are black-and-white design templates for each of the projects at the back of the book which can be traced from the page. These can be enlarged with a photocopier and adapted to suit other pieces of furniture.

Position the tracing on the surface, fix it with low tack tape and slide the transfer paper underneath, making sure that the active side is *facing down* (this is a common mistake!). You must slide the carbon under after the tracing paper has been placed to make sure that the pattern is in the correct position. Go over the outlines with a stylus, using enough pressure to leave the design on the surface. Don't press too hard or you will dent the wood.

The transferred lines are only an indication of where to paint. A sensitive or expressive stroke is always more effective than a 'filled in' look. Any lines left showing after painting should be erased.

PAINT TECHNIQUES

The techniques which follow show how to apply your newly learnt brushstrokes to create different effects with your painting.

Blocking in

Choose a brush size appropriate to the area that you are blocking in. Always start away from the edge of the outlines of the pattern. This way you won't get a ridge of paint building up where the two colours meet. Work towards the edges, using strokes that follow the shape of the area that you are blocking. By working slowly towards the line you will keep the definition of the line when painting the adjoining colour. If ridges of paint are formed as the paint squeezes out from the side of your loaded brush, it is too full. Wipe the excess off and run the brush back over the ridges to flatten and smooth them.

Cross hatching

Firstly to explain how you cross hatch with a long liner brush. The brush must travel smoothly across the surface, so load it well with paint, watered down to an inky consistency. Practise pulling the brush in lines towards you to build up a rhythmic stroke to produce an even series of lines. Turn the paper and repeat in the other direction to produce the cross hatching effect (see Lace book box on page 96).

An unusual background effect can be created using a flat brush. Pick up the base colour and a little white on a flat brush. Using short, random cutting strokes criss-cross the paint on to the background, alternating the strokes with lighter and darker shades of the background colour.

Dry brush

This technique can be used for highlighting or shading. Dip the brush in retarder and blot off the surplus moisture. Load the brush with paint and wipe it off on a tissue with a stroking motion until there is virtually nothing left on the brush. Lightly stroke the brush on to the surface and slowly build up the intensity of colour. Remember it is better to have too little paint on the brush than too much.

Fly specking

This technique of splashing dots of paint on a surface emulates the specks often seen on old paintings or furniture. Use a stipple brush or an old toothbrush. Mix a little Burnt Umber with some water to an inky consistency, dip the brush in this mix, tap off the excess moisture and using your nail, pull back along the bristles letting them flick the paint on to your project piece. Practise to see how much paint is coming off the bristles and how close the brush should be to the surface.

Push/pull technique

This technique is used for defining the edges of petals. For example, when painting a poppy petal using Orange Light as the primary colour and defining it with Alizarin Crimson. Using a round brush loaded with Orange Light and generously tip loaded with Alizarin Crimson, drizzle the Alizarin Crimson approximately 3-4 stroke widths along the edge of the petal or leaf to be painted. Then quickly wipe the excess Alizarin Crimson from the tip of the brush on a tissue.

The brush should still be full of the Orange Light. Now use comma strokes to fill in the petal. Start the comma just beneath the drizzled line of the Alizarin Crimson. Gently push the brush forward into the Alizarin Crimson so that the tip of the brush just catches a little and then pull back with the normal comma stroke. This should leave the ridge of paint but pull a little Alizarin Crimson down the petal.

Shading

There are two methods of shading. One is to use a darker colour or shade, side loaded on a clean, flat brush. This is blended on the palette by gradually walking the brush into the colour and back out again. The far edge must have absolutely no paint on it. This can be used around the edges of a petal to create a gradual increase in the intensity of colour on the edge fading away to nothing at the centre. The edge of the brush (side loaded with Burnt Umber) can be used below the outer edge of the petal to create a shadow. The second method for shading is to load first a flat brush with your main colour and then, on one side, load a darker shade of the main colour and blend them together on the palette. This creates a subtle blending of colour which is ideal for flesh tones, roses or leaves.

Tinting

This effect is achieved by watering down the colour you wish to use as a tint to a very thin wash. Load the brush with this wash then rest it on a tissue until the shine disappears. Stroke the colour lightly in the area, gradually building up the intensity of colour. If a little dot of water appears at the end of the stroke, the brush is too wet, in which case blot and try again.

Washes, glazing and floating colour

These techniques are used to overlay part or all of your project with a clear layer of colour through which the underlying work can be seen. They can also be used to shade under a flower or add subtle touches of highlight and shade to petals. The three methods are equally successful. I use all three, but tend to avoid using retarder as I like to work quickly and it takes a while to dry.

Washes

A wash is created by thinning paint down to various degrees of transparency with water.

Glazes

A glaze is paint thinned with a clear glazing medium, varnish or retarder to the required transparency - the same effect as floating colour.

Floating colour

This is the method of applying a transparent coat of paint by floating it on a surface which has been dampened with either a thin layer of water or retarder. This allows time to work the colour before it dries. Retarder keeps the paint workable for a longer period, but be careful to let it dry thoroughly before attempting a second coat. A side loaded flat brush is appropriate to float a transparent colour over this film. This is a good method to use on large areas where more than one stroke may be needed as it gives more time for blending out brushmarks. Floating is a skill which needs practice, but is an effective technique and worth developing.

Mistakes

There are ways of rescuing mistakes with paint. If you see immediately that you have made a mistake, a damp cloth or baby wipe will remove it. If it has dried, a little methylated spirits or alcohol on a cotton bud should remove the paint – however, beware not to damage the background paint. Leave to dry and paint over.

PAINT EFFECTS

When experimenting with the paint effects which follow, make up a large card for each effect with strips of your favourite background colours. Then apply the effects across them. This will give you an instant reference of colour variations for each paint effect.

Sponging

Natural sea sponges are excellent for this technique; they are much softer than manufactured ones, and have an irregular structure. Different sponges will give you a variety of effects according to their size and texture. Effects also depend on how hard you press the sponge on your project. You can gently pat the sponge up and down on the area for a fine, stippled effect, or slightly roll your wrist as you press down on to the project piece which can be striking when used with a marble mix, as it pushes the colours into each other. To keep your marine sponge in good condition, always wet it and squeeze it out before dipping it into any paint. Wash it out as soon as you have finished to keep it in good condition.

A simple masking method when sponging is to cut a piece of paper in the shape to be masked off, spray with removable mounting and fix in position. Do not soak the paper as this is a temporary measure.

Stippling

Stippling is a method of patting paint on to an area to give a soft, fuzzy look and it can be used as a background. Deer foot stippler brushes, small marine sponges or an artists' oil brush chopped off at the end are all good for this purpose. Load your brush or sponge with a watery mix of paint and pat the excess off on a piece of paper until the sponge or brush gives a speckled effect. You will then have the right amount of paint to start work (see Cockerel plaque on page 56).

Antiquing

This is a finishing effect combined with a colour which gives the surface an antique look. Before starting this process, make sure that the paint is completely dry. If it is cool to touch there will be remaining moisture. A hair-dryer can speed the drying process, but be careful not to burn your work by holding it too close. Make sure that all remaining chalk lines have been erased from your project. Instructions for mixing the antiquing medium are as follows:

1 Use 3-parts white spirit to 1-part raw linseed oil. Make up a reasonable amount of this antiquing medium in a jar as it can be put aside for future use. This can be used with any artists' oil paint colour, but Burnt Umber traditionally creates the impression of yellowing with age.

2 Squeeze out an inch of your Burnt Umber artists' oil paint on a small dish. Add some of the medium and mix to a soft, creamy paste.

3 Use a soft, lint-free cloth (old T-shirt fabric is ideal) or a brush and spread this mix over your project. **Don't panic** as the painting disappears! The linseed oil keeps the solution workable, giving you time to achieve the right look. Just keep going, making sure that you push the antiquing mix into any corners. Actual antique objects are always darker in the corners and grooves where dust, waxing and cleaning has

Chapter 2
ROUND BRUSH

This chapter concentrates on the basic strokes traditionally used for decorative painting. A variety of projects have been designed incorporating these simple techniques to gradually build up your decorative painting skills. Combined with the range of paint effect backgrounds, these simple brushstroke designs will allow you to give a new lease of life to furniture or wooden blanks.

Blue and white tulip table

This simple but effective design is an ideal project for beginners. Remember that simple designs can be just as successful as more intricate work. I have used crackle varnish and antiquing paint effects, but the design would look equally striking with fresh paint colours.

MATERIALS

Round brush No. 6

5 cm/2 in. sponge brush

5 cm/2 in. household paint brush

Varnishing brush

Soft make-up brush

Art carbon

Low tack tape

Stylus

Tracing paper

Hair-dryer

Antiquing medium

Crackle varnish

Oil-based varnish

Colour palette

Antique White

Antique Blue

Payne's Grey artists' oil paint

INSTRUCTIONS

1 **Background** Using a 5 cm/2 in. sponge brush paint the surface of the table and base with 2-3 coats of Antique White.

2 **Trace the pattern** Position and fix your traced pattern on the table with the tape. Slide the carbon underneath, making sure that the carbon side is facing down. Using the stylus, trace the outlines using enough pressure to leave the design on the surface without denting the wood.

3 **Tulips** Load the No. 6 brush with Antique Blue and tip load this with Antique White. Using the Comma and 'S' strokes paint in the tulips and leaves (see the worksheet on page 41 for the build up of the design). Once the paint is dry, erase any visible pattern lines.

4 **Crackle varnish** Using the household paint brush apply an even coat of the oil-based first stage of the crackle varnish over the whole surface of the table top and base. Leave to dry until it feels slightly tacky when you press your finger quite hard on the surface. Then give it the second water-based coat (see page 17).

As this is difficult to see, go over the surface in one direction (i.e. up and down) and then in the opposite direction (i.e. back and forth). It is important to make sure that you have covered the entire oil-based first coat. Any patches which are missed at this stage will become flat, brown patches when you antique the surface. The size of the cracks depends on how thickly you apply this second coat but be careful as too much will cause wrinkles.

5 **Antiquing** After leaving this to dry for two to three hours, apply direct heat to the surface with a hair-dryer which will encourage the surface to craze. To stabilise the crackles and heighten the crazing effect, antique the table top (see page 16 for full instructions). As the project is a blue colour, use Payne's Grey instead of Burnt Umber with the antiquing medium. Using a soft, lint-free cloth, spread your antique mix over the surface.

Start to buff off the excess using a soft, lint-free cloth. Use a circular motion, releasing the pressure as you work out towards the edge.

Buff over the surface with a soft glazing mop to make sure that there are no smears. If little stars of excess antiquing mix appear

where a few lines cross, remove with a cotton bud moistened with white spirit.

6 **Sealing** Seal the surface of the table with an oil-based varnish. This is very important as a water-based varnish will dissolve the crackle glaze. An alternative is to leave the piece for 7-10 days and wipe off the water-based glaze, leaving behind the fine lines of the Payne's Grey antique mix. Finally, apply the varnish.

Tip Practise crackle varnishing and antiquing on colour cards until you are confident you can achieve the finishes you require.

The two outer petals are 'S' strokes with their tails extended to meet at the base.

The centre petal consists of two comma strokes and an exclamation stroke overlapping each other.

Sunflower platter

These bold sunflowers are another good exercise for beginners. The size of the project will allow those of you who are just starting out to really go to town with lots of flamboyant 'S' strokes. Try to freehand the second layer of petals as it is just a matter of popping in random 'S' strokes over the first layer.

MATERIALS

Round brush No. 6

Deer foot stippler No. 6

7 cm/3 in. foam brush

Varnishing brush

Marine sponge

Art carbon

Chalk pencil

Low tack tape

Damp cloth

Retarder

Stylus

Tracing paper

Water spray or atomizer

Satin varnish

Colour palette

Russian Blue

Cerulean Blue

Antique White

Pale Lavender

Cobalt Blue

Hooker's Green

Burnt Umber

Cadmium Orange

Cadmium Yellow

Yellow Oxide

Yellow Light

Blue and Pale Lavender. Work the colours into the sponge and quickly apply to the surface.

Before the paint dries, use a water spray to moisten the platter until the colours begin to run.

INSTRUCTIONS

1 **Basecoat** Paint the platter with 1-2 coats of Russian Blue using the foam brush.

2 Using a damp cloth, wipe a thin film of retarder or water over the whole surface.

3 Dip a thoroughly dampened marine sponge into a marble mix of Cerulean Blue, Cobalt

4   When dry, give it one thin coat of satin varnish.

5   Transfer the pattern

6   **Leaves**   Block in the background of the leaves with a mix of Hooker's Green and Yellow Oxide on a No. 6 round brush. When this has dried, use a chalk pencil to indicate the centre of the leaf. Load the brush with Hooker's Green, tip loaded with Yellow Oxide. Using comma strokes, start from the base of the centre of the leaf and pull the commas out over the edge of the blocked-in leaves. Use a little more Yellow Oxide on one side of the leaf to indicate light coming from one side.

7   **Sunflowers**   Load the round brush with Yellow Oxide mixed with a little Cadmium Orange and tip loaded with Antique White and paint the background petals with 'S' strokes. Paint the top layer of petals freehand with Yellow Oxide, mixed with Yellow Light and tip loaded with Antique White. Do not paint in the petals that overlap the centre at this point.

8   Using the deer foot stippler, stipple the centre of the sunflowers with Burnt Umber so that it just overlaps the base of the petals. With a little Yellow Oxide on the front tip of the deer foot stippler, define the inner part of the centre circle. A small amount of Hooker's Green can be stippled into the centre of the flower.

9   Load the No. 6 round brush with the mix of Yellow Oxide and Cadmium Yellow and tip load with White, then add the small petals that curl over the centres.

10 **Finishing**   Give the platter 2-3 coats of satin varnish.

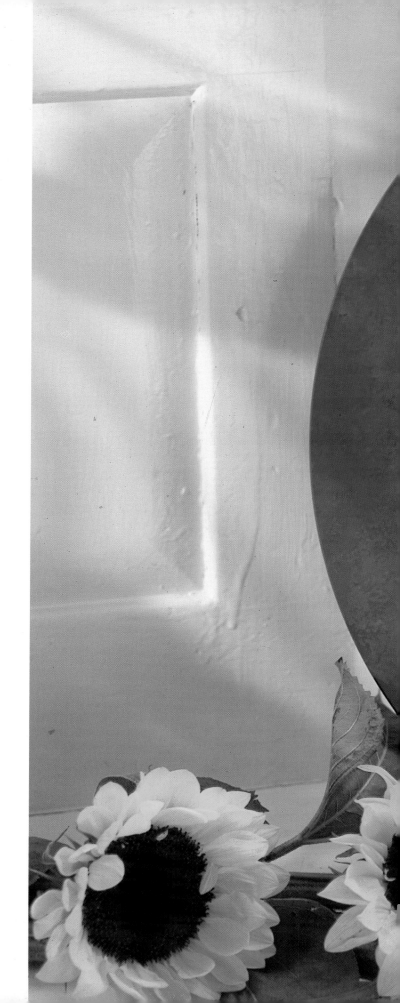

Daisy chair

This chair was inspired by a picture of Monet's kitchen in Giverny which showed the vibrant yellow and blue painted furniture glowing magically in the warm sunlight.

MATERIALS

Round brush No. 4

Make-up sponge

Varnishing brush

Art carbon

Fine sandpaper/brown paper bag

Low tack tape

Stylus

Tracing paper

Satin varnish

Colour palette

Parisian Yellow

Ultramarine Blue

Antique White

the sponge astride the corner, draw it straight along the edge in one swift movement.

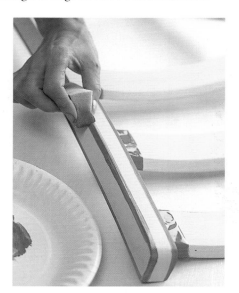

INSTRUCTIONS

1 **Background** Use a small brush to touch in the paint around the joints and spindles before using a make-up sponge to colour the whole background Parisian Yellow. Make-up sponges are ideal for this as they spread the paint very smoothly and easily on chair legs and spindles. Once the chair is dry, sand the surface with a fine sandpaper or buff with a brown paper bag before applying a second coat.

2 Mask the areas where the cross bands meet the back joints of the chair. Apply the lines of the blue border to the chair back and legs by dipping a small wedge of make-up sponge into a pale mix of Ultramarine Blue and Antique White. Dab off excess paint and then, placing

3 Transfer the pattern to the chair.

4 **Daisies** Use a pale mix of Ultramarine Blue and Antique White, tip loaded with Antique White on a No. 4 round brush. Use the comma stroke technique to paint in the daisies (see page 31) and scrolls on the chair sides and back. When the paint is dry, use a soft eraser to clean off any remaining traced lines.

5 Seal your work with 2-3 coats of satin varnish which can also be applied with a make-up sponge.

Rose magazine rack

The design on this magazine rack was inspired by the garlands of roses and tulips which are characteristic of Regency painted furniture. I have created this project using simple comma and 'S' strokes to show just how effective they can be. These elements combine to create a sophisticated and striking design.

MATERIALS

Round brush No. 4

Marine sponge

7 cm/3 in. sponge brush

Varnishing brush

Art carbon

Low tack tape

Stylus

Tracing paper

Crackle glaze

Satin varnish

Colour palette

Antique White

Antique Green

Hooker's Green

Yellow Oxide

Ultramarine Blue

Plum

Persian Rose

INSTRUCTIONS

1 **Basecoat** Using the sponge brush paint the magazine rack with pale Antique Green.

2 Use the design template to mark the area you wish to crackle glaze.

3 Paint the area under the garlands with the crackle glaze and leave to dry. Combine some Antique White into a wash with 2-parts water and 1-part satin varnish. Work the wash into a damp marine sponge on the palette. With a rolling movement cover the crackle glaze with this mix. Be careful not to go over the same area twice, for as soon as the paint comes into contact with the crackle glaze the chemical reaction will start. If you make a mistake, wipe the surface off with a damp cloth and leave to dry before starting again (see page 18).

4 **Transfer the design** Having ensured that the surface is completely dry, the next stage is to trace the flower pattern on to the magazine rack.

5 **Leaves** Mix a pale green colour using Hooker's Green, Yellow Oxide and Antique White. Load the No. 4 round brush and use the 'S' stroke to form the rose leaves and highlight them with Antique White. A paler version of this green, tip loaded with Antique White can be used for the small leaves which are just small, fat 'S' strokes. Add more White as you work towards the tips of the garlands which will give the impression that the leaves are fading into the background.

6 **Roses** Mix a pale pink with Persian Rose and Antique White. Load the No. 4 brush with pink, then flatten and side load with Antique White on one side and Persian Rose on the other. Paint in the three back petals using little half comma strokes. Dab the centres of the roses with a brush loaded with Yellow Oxide, back loaded with Persian Rose and tip loaded

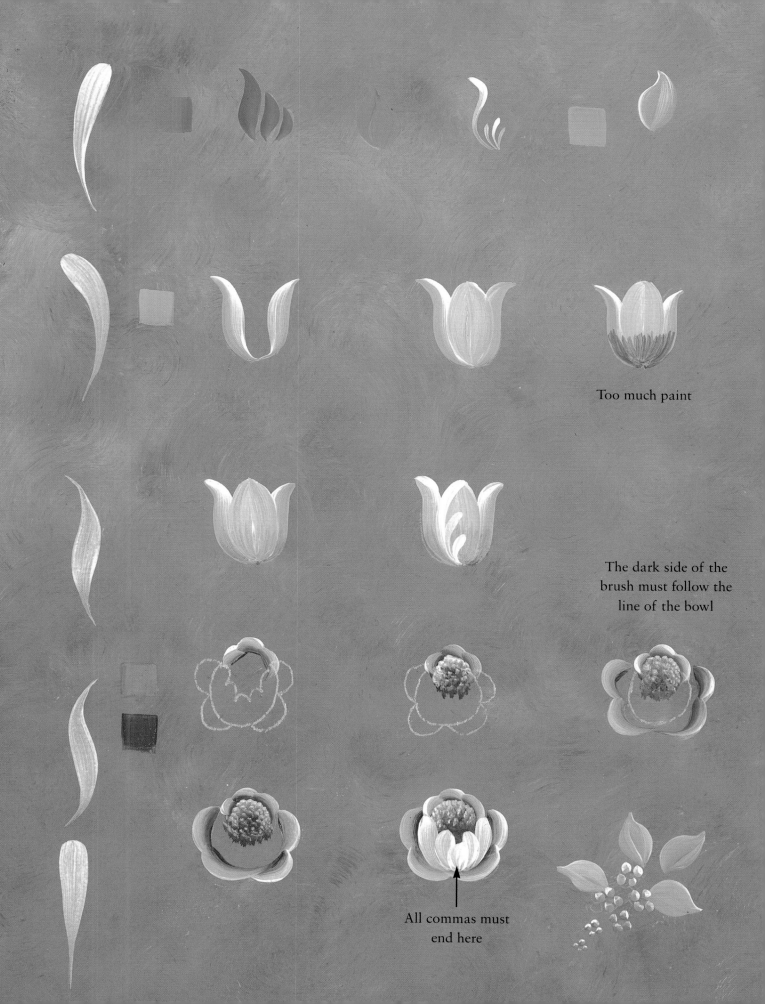

Too much paint

The dark side of the
brush must follow the
line of the bowl

All commas must
end here

with Antique White. The outer petals must follow the line of the bowl of the rose. Concentrate on the side of the brush with the Persian Rose, making sure it follows the line of the bowl. The other side will take care of itself. The brush is not flattened for the commas which make up the bowl of the rose – just use a round brush loaded with pink and tip loaded with Antique White.

7 Tulips Load the No. 4 brush with Yellow Oxide lightened with Antique White, tip load with Antique White and paint the outer petals with 'S' strokes and the centre petals with comma strokes. The blush at the base of the tulip is achieved using a tinting technique (see page 15). Water down the Persian Rose colour, resting the brush on a tissue until all the excess water drains out. Stroke the base of the rose very lightly, gradually building up the intensity of colour. If any dots of water appear at the end of the stroke, the brush is too wet.

8 Forget-me-nots Make a marble mix of Plum, Ultramarine Blue and Antique White. With a No. 4 brush, pick up varying proportions of colour so that some flowers are more plum coloured and others, more pale blue. With this mix still on the brush, kick load Antique White on the tip. The forget-me-nots will be highlighted on one side when you put the brush down. Make sure that there is enough paint on the brush so that the tip load of paint touches the surface, creating perfect, round dots. Insufficient paint will result in paw prints.

9 Varnishing It is essential to be quick with the first coat of varnish over the crackled area, as the paint over the crackle glaze may soften and smudge. Alternatively you could spray varnish the piece.

Experiment on paper until you can paint directly and confidently on the clock. Any mistakes can be removed with a damp cloth.

An alternative is to define the circle by freehand with small commas and/or dots. The numbers of the dial are painted using a No. 2 round brush loaded with Antique White.

4 Transfer the design starting with the ribbon, cosmos flowers and leaves. The other motifs should be added after these are painted as many of the small flowers should overlay the leaves.

5 **Ribbon** Load a No. 4 round brush with an apricot mix of Antique White with a dash of Yellow Oxide and Alizarin Crimson. Side load with Antique White.

6 **Leaves** With the No. 4 round brush, paint the leaves using the 'S' stroke. Antique Green is used for the larger leaves and a paler shade for the stems and small leaves. To paint the leaf curl, load the brush with Leaf Green and side tip load with Antique White using the wave stroke (see page 23). The decorative comma strokes on the leaves are a pale mix of Antique Green. The small flicked leaves are pale Antique Green, tip loaded with Antique White.

7 **Cosmos flowers** Each of the flowers is a variation of the apricot colour used for the ribbon. Just add a little more White, Red or Yellow to the mix as you move to each flower so that no two are exactly alike. The paint should be mixed to a watery consistency to give the flowers a translucent look. Paint in the cosmos flowers with the No. 4 brush using the push and pull technique (see page 14). Starting from the centre, tint the base of the petals with a transparent wash of Leaf Green (see page 15). Stipple the stamens with Yellow Oxide and then highlight with a little White over the top of the stamens and Burnt Sienna at the base of the stamens to create shadow. Use the wave stroke to add the petal curl.

8 Trace the rest of the pattern.

9 **Lavender daisies** Paint the daisies using a No. 2 brush with Antique White and a dash of Cobalt Blue and Alizarin Crimson, tip loaded with Antique White. Vary the flower colour by adding a little more Red or Blue. The centres are stippled with Yellow Oxide.

10 **White bells** Use a No. 2 round brush loaded with Antique White and paint the white bells using two small comma strokes with flicked up tails. Add three small stamens.

11 **Yellow flowers** Load the No. 4 round brush with Yellow Oxide kick loaded with Antique White. Keeping the white facing the top of the clock, dot in the petals.

12 **Forget-me-nots** Load a marble mix of Antique Blue and Antique White on the No. 4 round brush. Dot in the petal and then add the centres with Yellow Oxide.

13 Using a No. 2 brush, add some small decorative commas to the design with Leaf Green, tip loaded with Antique White.

14 **Finishing** Apply 2-3 coats of satin varnish.

Flip the white to
alternate sides

Push into the white
and pull down

Tint the centre leaf green

Stipple the base

Leave space for the
petal to turn over

Stipple the highlight

Stipple the shadow

Cockerel plaque

This cockerel was inspired by an old naïve painting. I wonder if there is such a thing as naïve carpentry? If there is, perhaps my simplistic attempts come into this category! The kitchen tidy is made from left-over, rough-sawn pieces of wood. In keeping with the rustic style, the wood was not sealed.

MATERIALS

Flat brush No. 10

Round brushes
No. 2, 4, 6

Fine marine sponge

Varnishing brush

Art carbon

Low tack tape

Tracing paper

Stylus

Satin varnish

Colour palette

Burnt Sienna

Bold Red

Raw Sienna

Ocean Green

Yellow Oxide

Hooker's Green

Black

INSTRUCTIONS

1 Stain the raw wood with a wash of Raw Sienna.

2 Lightly stipple the front with watery mixes of Raw Sienna, followed by Burnt Sienna with random touches of Hooker's Green.

3 Side load and palette blend the No. 10 flat brush with Burnt Sienna and use this to add a few streaks at ground level for the tufts of dry grass to grow from. Add the tufts with a No. 2 round brush loaded with pale Yellow Oxide.

4 **Border** Load a No. 10 flat shader with a wash of Black to stain the cross bars and edges.

5 **Cockerel** Transfer the cockerel design. With a No. 6 round brush, block in the comb, wattle, front of the neck and chest in Bold Red. The back, tail and wings are Ocean Green and the legs and feet are Black.

6 **Feathers** Load the No. 6 round brush with Ocean Green, tip loaded with Black, and starting at the tip of the tail, paint in the feathers using sweeping strokes. Using the No. 6 round brush, indicate the feathers on the neck, chest and wings with a glaze of translucent Black.

7 **Beak** Load a No. 2 round brush with Yellow Oxide and outline with Black. The nostril is indicated with a Black comma stroke. Add a little shading to the comb by mixing Burnt Sienna with Bold Red. The eye is made up of a large dot of Black with a smaller dot of Yellow Oxide in the centre and an even smaller dot of Black in its centre.

8 **Border** Paint the border using comma strokes with a No. 4 round brush loaded with Yellow Oxide.

9 **Finishing** Apply 2-3 coats of satin varnish to finish. The piece can be hung with a rough string which has been soaked in black tea to discolour it.

Chapter 3
FLAT BRUSH

Flat brush strokes and blending techniques are used in this chapter in conjunction with the round brush work you have covered in the previous chapter. Here the flat brush is principally used with side loading and palette blending techniques to bring greater depth and subtle highlights to your work. Your painting skills will continue to develop as you learn to incorporate stroke work using the ruffle technique and a variety of brush loading and blending techniques.

Pansy hat box

I was inspired to paint these pansies after a visit to a market where a stallholder had brought the first plants for Spring. After the grey of winter, their vibrant colours seemed quite dazzling. This project focuses on the blending of paint, so it may be appropriate to use the floating technique (see page 15).

MATERIALS

Round brushes No. 2, 4

Flat brushes No. 8, 10

Detail brush 0/10

Marine sponge

Sponge brush

Varnishing brush

Art carbon

Low tack tape

Retarder

Stylus

Tracing paper

Satin varnish

Colour palette

Russian Blue

Indigo

Raw Umber

Antique White

Yellow Oxide

Ocean Green

Hooker's Green

Cadmium Yellow

Persian Rose

Pale Lavender

Burnt Umber

Leaf Green

Burgundy

Purple Dioxide

Burnt Umber artists' oil paint

INSTRUCTIONS

1   Give the hat box a basecoat of Russian Blue.

2   **Background** Roughly mark the area on the lid and base to be sponged. Create a marble mix of Indigo and Antique White and work this mix with a damp marine sponge. Sponge the lid and base, alternately picking up a little more white or dark blue. Create a wavy edge to divide the plain background from the paint effect. If you use the paints undiluted, the surface will have a slightly textured finish.

3   When the surface is dry, lightly sponge a few drifts of a Raw Umber wash.

4   Transfer the design.

5   **Ribbon** Use the No. 4 round brush loaded with a mid-yellow (Yellow Oxide and Antique White), side loaded with Antique White. Water down the paints so that you get a good sweep. Small holes may appear over the textured surface but this just adds to the distressed effect.

6   **Highlights** Paint the highlight on the ribbon with a No. 8 flat brush. It may be easier to float the paint over a thin layer of water or retarder (see page 10). Side load and palette blend the flat brush with Antique White. With the white side facing the centre of the area to be highlighted, stroke the side loaded brush across the ribbon, then flip the brush over and repeat, butting the white edge to the white edge. Repeat these strokes working away from the centre to create a gradual fading of the highlight. (Alternatively, the dry brush

technique is an effective way of painting highlights – see page 14.)

7 Leaves Load the No. 8 flat brush with Ocean Green and side load on one corner with Yellow Oxide and on the other with Hooker's Green. Blend on the palette and apply the ruffle stroke leaves. Start at the base of the leaf with the brush in the horizontal position. Press down, and zig-zag the brush down one side of the leaf with the Yellow Oxide to the side from which you want the light to come. As you near the tip of the leaf, gradually release the pressure until you are up on the chisel edge. At this point gently roll the brush between your finger and thumb bringing it round to a vertical position on its chisel edge. Then lift off, sweeping the stroke to a point. Flip the brush over and with the Yellow Oxide butting the Hooker's Green, repeat down the other side of the leaf.

8 Add shadow to the base of the leaves that are tucked under the lower petals of the pansy. Float the colour on to the surface (see page 15). Use the No. 8 flat brush, side loaded and blended with Burnt Umber, and float a thin shade of paint on to the base of the leaves (with the dark side of the brush facing the edge of the petals). Use the No. 2 round brush loaded with Hooker's Green and side tip loaded with Leaf Green to add curled edges to the tips of the leaves with the wave stroke (see page 23).

9 Pansies and buds With a No. 4 round brush, paint a basecoat on the first and third pansies and the buds in pale yellow made up from Antique White and Yellow Oxide. The second pansy and its bud should be painted in Pale Lavender. Two or three coats may be needed.

All the petals for the pansies are edged using the ruffle technique. The three different pansies are numbered according to the design template on page 123.

Pansy No. 1 Side load a No. 10 flat brush with Antique White and edge the petals using the ruffle technique (see page 27). Then clean the brush and side load it with a mix of Burgundy and Burnt Umber and use the ruffle technique to shade the centre. With the detail brush, add the little beard in the centre of the flowers in Yellow Oxide.

Pansy No. 2 Side load the No. 10 flat brush with Purple Dioxide and edge the four upper petals using the ruffle technique. The bottom petal should then be edged in Pale Lavender side loaded with Antique White. Side load the brush with Purple Dioxide and shade the centre using the ruffle technique. With the detail brush, add the little beard in the centre of the flowers in Yellow Oxide.

Pansy No. 3 Side load the No. 10 flat brush with Burgundy to which has been added a touch of Burnt Umber. Edge the top petals using the ruffle technique. Then edge the lower three petals with Cadmium Yellow. Overglaze with a narrow band of shading in Persian Rose. Side load the brush with a mix of Burgundy and Burnt Umber and add the centre shading with the ruffle technique. Using a detail brush, add the little beard in the centre in Yellow Oxide.

10 Finishing Erase any remaining pattern lines and lightly antique the surface with Burnt Umber. Leave to dry and varnish after 7-10 days.

Poppy bread bin

When I found this old enamel flour bin, it was looking quite sad with chipped edges. Rather than restore it, I decided to make a feature of its rather worn, rustic look. It was going to be used as a bread bin so I incorporated the golden tones of baked bread with the poppies and cornflowers once so much a part of cornfields.

MATERIALS

Round brushes
No. 2, 4, 6

Flat brush No. 8

2 cm/¾ in. flat brush

5 cm/2 in. sponge brush

Detail brush

Small, fine marine sponge

Soft make-up brush

Varnishing brush

Art carbon

Low tack tape

Stylus

Damp cloth

Retarder

Cocktail stick

Tracing paper

Water spray/atomizer

PVA glue

Antiquing medium

Satin varnish

Colour palette

Antique White

Antique Green

Hooker's Green

Yellow Oxide

Yellow Light

Burnt Sienna

Raw Sienna

Burnt Umber

Alizarin Crimson

Orange Light

Burgundy

Ultramarine Blue

Cobalt Blue

Plum

Burnt Umber artists' oil colour

INSTRUCTIONS

1 **Preparation** When dealing with enamel, make sure that it is cleaned thoroughly (see page 12). Paint the surface with PVA glue mixed with a little water (1-part PVA to 2-3 parts water). Once dry, this will give a good key for the background colour.

2 Using the sponge brush paint a basecoat of Antique White.

3 Wipe the surface of the bread bin with a damp cloth and, while still damp, sponge the surface with a loose marble mix of Raw Sienna and Antique White. Lightly spray with water when working to make the colours blur into each other.

4 Initially, just trace the scroll on to the bread bin.

5 **Scroll** Using the flat brush, block in the scroll with one or two coats of Antique White. If you only use one coat, the shadows of the undercoat create a parchment effect. Use straight, sweeping strokes across the area. Side load and palette blend the 2 cm/¾ in. flat brush with Raw Sienna and add the shading to the inside edges of the scroll. The Raw Sienna should be blended three-quarters of the way

across the brush. If you want more definition, this process can be repeated with Burnt Umber one-quarter of the way across the brush. Use the No. 2 round brush with Burnt Umber to outline the tears in the scroll. Use a mix of the background colour to paint in the tears.

6 When dry, transfer the remaining design.

7 Letters Load a No. 4 round brush with Raw Sienna and tip load with Antique White. Use simple 'S' strokes to form the letters.

8 Leaves With a mix of Hooker's Green and Yellow Oxide loaded on a No. 2 round brush, add the small leaves, flower stems and broken grasses in the background. Paint over the small traced flowers which will be filled in later. With this mix loaded on a No. 4 round brush, paint in the large poppy leaves using comma and 'S' strokes. With the green still on the brush, side tip load with Antique White and edge the poppy leaves with the wave stroke. The same method is used for the cornflower leaves which are painted using Antique Green and Antique White.

9 Corn Paint in the corn using a No. 2 round brush with a marble mix of Burnt Sienna, Raw Sienna and Antique White.

10 Lily-of-the-valley Paint the flowers using a No. 2 round brush loaded with Antique White.

11 Daisies Paint the mauve daisies with a No. 2 brush loaded with Plum and tip loaded with Antique White. The centres are Orange Light stippled with Yellow Light. The white daisies are Antique White with Yellow Light centres.

12 Poppies Paint the poppies using the No. 6 round brush. First load the brush with Orange Light, generously tip loaded with Alizarin Crimson. Drizzle a ragged line with Alizarin Crimson approximately 3-4 stroke widths along the edge of the petal and quickly wipe the excess Alizarin Crimson off the tip of the brush. The brush should still be full of the Orange Light. Using the push/pull technique use comma strokes to fill in the petals. Start the comma just beneath the drizzled line of Alizarin Crimson. Gently push the brush forward into the Alizarin Crimson so that the tip of the brush just catches a little and then pull back with the normal comma stroke. This should leave a ridge of the Alizarin Crimson paint but also pull some of the colour down the petal.

To highlight the petals, dip the brush in retarder and dab off the excess (see page 10). Load with Orange Light and wipe off on a tissue with a stroking motion until there is very little paint left. Stroke the highlight on to the petal, slowly building up the intensity. It is always better to have too little on the brush than too much for dry brush work.

13 Stamens Blot in the centres of the poppies with the No. 4 round brush loaded with Yellow Oxide and tip loaded with Burnt Umber. Use a stylus to add Burnt Umber dots over the centre. Paint the centre of the poppy bud with the No. 4 round brush loaded with Orange Light and tipped with Alizarin Crimson. The calyx is painted the same colour as the poppy leaves. The fine hairs are added with a size 10/0 detail brush.

14 Cornflowers Define the base of the flowers with little dots of Cobalt Blue which are an indication of where to start the clusters of petals which are characteristic of cornflowers. Load a No. 8 flat brush with Ultramarine Blue, side loaded with Antique White. Using the chisel edge of your flat brush, stipple little fans of petals, keeping the Ultramarine Blue to the base of the petal. When you have completed the back row of petals, use a fine marine sponge fixed to a cocktail stick to stipple the centre of the flower (see page 11). Stipple first with a layer of Pale Ultramarine Blue, then Ultramarine Blue and finally, Burgundy. Add the front rows of petals using the same method as the back.

15 Finishing Antique the surface with Burnt Umber and satin varnish after 10 days.

Lion book box

The inspiration for this project which uses an aged, leather look was inspired by heraldic designs, where the tradition of decorative painting was once the preserve of men.

MATERIALS

Round brushes No. 2, 4

0/5 liner brush

2 cm/¾ in. flat brush

5 cm/2 in. sponge brush

5 cm/2 in. coarse household paint brush

Marine sponge

Art carbon

Tracing paper

Low tack tape

Fine sandpaper/000 steel wool

Antiquing medium

Crackle glaze

Satin varnish

Colour palette

Terracotta

Spruce Green

Antique White

Antique Gold

Bold Red

Burnt Umber

Yellow Oxide

Titanium White

Burnt Umber artists' oil colour

INSTRUCTIONS

1 Using a sponge brush, paint the book box with a basecoat of Terracotta inside and out (except the pages, which are Antique White).

2 **Front cover** Apply a coat of crackle glaze to the front cover. When the glaze is dry, sponge over the surface with Spruce Green paint and leave to crackle.

3 **Back cover** Sponge a second thick layer of Terracotta generously on the back and spine of the book. This will create an uneven surface and help to give the impression of leather. When this is dry, paint over in Spruce Green using the sponge brush. When this coat has dried, take some fine sandpaper or 000 steel wool and rub over the green until the spots of the Terracotta start to show through.

4 **Pages** Paint the leaves of the book around the edge of the box in Antique White using the 2 cm/¾ in. flat brush. Make up a mix of 4-parts satin varnish to 1-part Antique Gold with a dash of Burnt Umber. Working one side at a time, apply this mix and quickly drag your coarse household brush across the surface, creating an impression of book leaves (see the step-by-step photographs on page 96).

5 Trace the outline of the lion on the front cover.

6 **Lion** Block in the lion with Yellow Oxide loaded on a No. 4 round brush (it may need 2-3 coats). Then give it a top coat of Antique Gold. When dry, trace the detail of the face and fur on to the lion's body. Paint the eye Titanium White with a No. 2 round brush and dot the centre with Burnt Umber. Paint the tongue and claws in Bold Red. Load the No. 2 round brush with Burnt Umber and outline the lion and tufts of fur. Mask off the centre panel of the front cover and frame it with gold paint.

7 **Finishing** Erase all chalk lines and antique with Burnt Umber.

Blackberry breadboard

The idea for painting this breadboard came to me whilst visiting Russia. I was fortunate enough to visit several typical country homes in which I saw decorated wooden items in everyday use – including bread and cheeseboards. For this project, only one side needs decoration as the other side is used to cut the bread. I created a wood stain effect by thinning the paint with water, thus allowing the grain of the wood to show through the design.

MATERIALS

Round brush No. 2

Detail brush 10/0

Flat brushes No. 4, 6

Varnishing brush

Art carbon (red)

Stylus

Tracing paper

Low tack tape

Retarder

Satin varnish/sealer

Colour palette

Yellow Oxide

Antique White

Hooker's Green

Burgundy

Terracotta

Persian Rose

Burnt Sienna

INSTRUCTIONS

1 Seal the wood with 2 thin coats of satin varnish or sealer.

2 **Transfer the design** A red carbon and very light pressure should be used as some of the carbon lines may be seen through the thin glaze of the paint.

3 Load a No. 2 round brush with Yellow Oxide and side tip load with Burnt Sienna, and paint in the stems (keeping the Burnt Sienna to the underside of the stems). With a detail brush, add the thorns using comma strokes.

4 **Leaves** Load the No. 6 flat brush with retarder and remove excess by resting the brush on a tissue until the sheen disappears. Load the brush with Hooker's Green one side and Yellow Oxide on the other and blend this well on the palette. The Yellow Oxide should blend right into the green to turn it a lighter shade. Paint in all the leaves using the ruffle stroke (see page 27).

  The veins of the leaves are added with the detail brush using a mix of Yellow Oxide and Hooker's Green. Side load the No. 6 flat brush with Persian Rose, blend to a fine glaze on the palette and randomly add a blush to some of the leaves.

5 **Blackberries** The berries towards the base of the stem are darker than those at the tip. With the No. 6 flat brush, basecoat the darker berries in a pale mix of Burgundy and Antique White. Wash the brush and side load with Burgundy, then define the cells with small 'C' strokes. Add emphasis to some of the cells by adding a little Purple Dioxide to the Burgundy. When dry, go over the whole berry with a wash of this mix.

Naïve clock

The idea for the pattern on this clock came from a wall panel painted by William Price in 1831 displayed in the Francis du Pont Winterthur Museum, USA. In the second quarter of the nineteenth century, there was a fashion for murals painted in shades of brown and green. I find the use of such a limited palette very appealing, where naïve motifs and a simple use of colour are combined with a carefully structured design.

MATERIALS

*Flat brushes
No. 8, 10, 18*

*Round brushes
No. 1, 2, 4*

Deer foot stippler No. 6

5 cm/2 in. sponge brush

Fine marine sponge

Varnishing brush

Art carbon (yellow)

Tracing paper

Stylus

Liquid masking

Low tack tape

Crackle glaze

Retarder

Satin varnish

Colour palette

Antique White

Antique Blue

Antique Green

Terracotta

Olive Green

Hooker's Green

Burnt Umber

Burnt Sienna

Raw Sienna

Payne's Grey

INSTRUCTIONS

1 Give the clock a basecoat of Antique White mixed with a touch of Olive Green.

2 Apply the crackle glaze to the whole of the clock and leave to dry.

3 Apply a wash of very pale Antique Blue over the crackle glaze, using a 5 cm/2 in. sponge brush (this is better than an ordinary brush as it holds more paint and makes it easier to travel across the surface before running out of paint). Use strokes that sweep from side to side across the clock. This uneven wash begins the effect of the sky and water.

4 Trace the pattern with yellow carbon which will not show through the washes. With a dark carbon, the lines will show through the washes and once under the paint, will not rub off.

5 **Water effect** Create a water effect for the lake using a No. 8 flat brush, side loaded with a thin wash of Antique Green. Use random strokes across the lake with the colour on the side pointing to the top of the clock. Repeat with Raw Sienna and Payne's Grey.

6 **Hills** Using a No. 18 flat brush loaded with a wash of Payne's Grey, Raw Sienna and Hooker's Green, paint the hills in the background with the strokes following the shape of the hills. When dry, go over them with a wash of Antique Green and Raw Sienna. Emphasize the outline of the hills by shading them using the same brush side loaded with a wash of Payne's Grey.

7 Fields Before painting in the background colours of the fields, apply liquid masking to the tree trunk to avoid building up too much depth of colour (see page 10). Finely stipple the fields outside the house using a fine marine sponge. Apply the paint in three layers, allowing the paint to dry in between each layer. Start with Raw Sienna. Then finely stipple with Hooker's Green and finally lightly stipple with Burnt Sienna. The field in the foreground was done in the same way but using more Burnt Sienna to make it darker. Using a No. 10 flat brush side loaded with a mix of Burnt Sienna and Burnt Umber, define the edge of the field in the background where it meets the water's edge. In the same way differentiate the foreground field from the background field and lake.

8 House Using a No. 18 flat brush loaded with Antique White, block in the walls. For the roof, use Payne's Grey.

9 Windows Side load and palette blend a No. 6 flat brush with Burnt Umber. The windows are indicated by shadows. Keeping the side load to the right side of the windows, stroke in the shadows so that they disappear on the left. The door is painted using Burnt Umber loaded all the way across the brush. Add the dormer window using a No. 1 round brush loaded with Burnt Umber.

10 Grass Mix Hooker's Green and Burnt Sienna on the No. 2 round brush and stroke in the tufts of grass.

11 Tree Peel off the masking and paint the bark of the tree. With a No. 4 round brush, stroke random washes of Burnt Sienna, Payne's Grey and Raw Sienna down the trunk and along the branches. If necessary use a No. 2 round brush for the finer branches.

12 Bushes and leaves To create the fine effect of leaves on the tree, water down a mix of Hooker's Green, Raw Sienna and Burnt Umber. Dip a No. 6 deer foot stippler into the paint, dab off the excess until almost dry and stipple the leaves. Use Antique Green for the bushes and accentuate with Hooker's Green.

13 Lady Paint the lady with a No. 1 round brush. The skin tones consist of a very pale mix of Terracotta and Antique White. The hair and shawl are painted in Burnt Sienna. The dress is a mix of Hooker's Green and Burnt Sienna. The frills on the dress are Burnt Umber. The angler, the man in the boat and the boat are all painted in Burnt Sienna.

14 Fence Paint using a No. 1 round brush loaded with Burnt Sienna.

15 The hours on the naïve clock can be indicated by small dots or triangles.

16 Finishing Lightly antique and then varnish.

Nautical lap desk

This ship was inspired by an old painting my husband had in his antique shop. You could adapt a picture of any ship into a design such as this. It really isn't difficult and I have broken it down into easy-to-follow steps.

MATERIALS

*Round brushes
No. 1, 2, 3, 4*

*Flat brushes No. 6, 8, 10
and 2 cm/¾ in.*

5/0 liner brush

1.3 cm/½ in. comb brush

5 cm/2 in. sponge brush

Varnishing brush

Art carbon

Tracing paper

Low tack tape

Stylus

*Fine sandpaper/000
steel wool*

Antiquing medium

Crackle glaze

Matt or satin varnish

Colour palette

Russian Blue

Antique White

Yellow Oxide

Raw Sienna

Cerulean Blue

Burnt Umber

Ocean Green

Antique Gold

Indigo

Alizarin Crimson

Terracotta

Hooker's Green

Payne's Grey

Burnt Sienna

*Burnt Umber artists'
oil colour*

INSTRUCTIONS

1 Basecoat Apply 2-3 coats of Russian Blue to the exterior and Terracotta to the interior using the sponge brush. The edges of the lid and base are painted Terracotta with Antique Gold applied roughly using your finger.

2 Only trace the outline of the centre panel and the flags which decorate the top and edges of the desk.

3 Centre panel Block in the centre panel with Antique White, using a No. 10 flat brush. Don't worry if it is not perfectly white as this will heighten its distressed appearance.

4 Crackle glaze Apply the crackle glaze using the 5 cm/2 in. sponge brush or a No. 8 flat brush to the centre panel, and the flags and scrolls decorating the lid and sides. Leave to dry (see page 17). When dry, apply a coat of Antique White which will then crackle. This can be applied either with a brush or a sponge. Remember not overstroke the crackle while it is wet as it will disturb the crazing.

5 Flags and scrolls With the No. 8 flat brush, paint the flags and scrolls decorating the lid and sides (see worksheet on page 85).

6 Sky Mark the horizon. Side load the 2 cm/¾ in. flat brush with a pale, sky blue wash of Cerulean Blue and Antique White. Starting at the top of the panel, with the blue side load pointing to the top, work your way down the panel. Sweep from side to side, allowing the paint to fade to almost nothing a third of the way down the sky. Side load the brush with a wash of Yellow Oxide and repeat

this technique, starting with the colour next to the horizon and working your way up to meet the pale blue of the sky.

7 Clouds Add a few random sweeps of an Ocean Green wash across the top half of the sky. Disturb the paint by rubbing it with your finger, using a circular motion. Repeat with Indigo, bringing the colour in from the corners. Add a little Antique White to the edge of the clouds, using your finger.

8 Sea Paint with a wash of Ocean Green using a 2 cm/¾ in. flat brush. Load the No. 10 flat brush with Hooker's Green and add the waves with a chopping action. Create shade beneath the ship by adding some Indigo. With a No. 5/0 liner brush, drizzle a little white across the top of some waves. Use a 2 cm/¾ in. comb brush to pull the white paint down the waves with a curving motion.

9 Trace the pattern of the ship and sails but do not trace any of the ropes or ladders yet.

10 Sails Using a 2 cm/¾ in. flat brush, block in the sails with Antique White (see page 14). Use a 5/0 liner brush loaded with Yellow Oxide to paint the seams on the sails. The telltales (ribbons sewn to the sail to indicate wind direction) are painted in Raw Sienna with a tiny dot of Indigo at the top. Side load and palette blend a 2 cm/¾ in. flat brush with a wash of Burnt Umber to shade the sails as indicated on the worksheet.

11 Ship Using a No. 2 round brush, paint the line on the side of the ship in Alizarin Crimson. Use a No. 6 flat brush loaded with Indigo to paint the main body of the ship.

12 Trace the rigging and all remaining details.

13 Masts and rigging Load a No. 1 round brush with Burnt Sienna, side tip loaded with Burnt Umber on one side and Yellow Oxide on the other. Paint in the masts, keeping the Burnt Umber to the left. The spars and the small people are painted with Burnt Umber. The cabin is Raw Sienna with a Burnt Sienna roof. The lifeboat is painted in Antique White. Using a No. 5/0 liner brush loaded with Indigo, add all the ropes and ladders, and outline the sails.

14 Flags on the ship Paint the background of the flags with Antique White, using a No. 1 round brush and then add decorative details (see worksheet on page 85).

15 The ships in the distance are indicated using a No. 6 flat brush loaded with a very pale mix of Payne's Grey and Antique White.

16 Frame The picture is framed using comma strokes painted with a No. 4 round brush, loaded with Terracotta and tip loaded with Antique Gold.

17 Finishing When completely dry, use very fine sandpaper (or 000 steel wool) over the desk to distress the edges and corners (which are most likely to have suffered the wear and tear of time). Erase any remaining traced lines, dust off and antique the lap desk with Burnt Umber. Leave for a few days before varnishing.

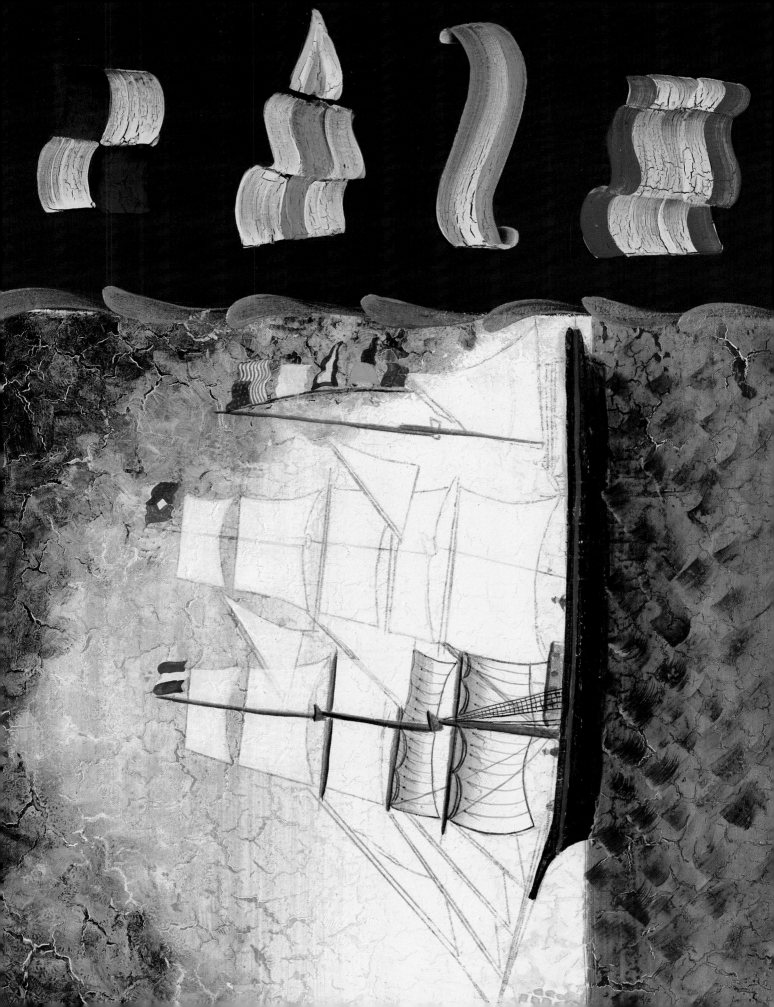

Chapter 4
CLASSIC PAINTING

The projects in this chapter bring
together a range of classic styles
influenced by Russian, early
American and French furniture,
and objets d'art. The designs use
all the different round and flat
brush techniques which you have
learnt in the previous chapters.

Rose and tulip tray

The design for the spray of flowers on this tray was influenced by the beautiful collection of eighteenth-century Sèvres porcelain which can be seen at the Wallace Collection in London. This small museum is a great source of inspiration and well worth a visit.

MATERIALS

Round brushes
No. 1, 2, 3

Flat brush No. 8

Detail brush 10/0

No. 4 deer foot stippler

5 cm/2 in. sponge brush

Marine sponge

Varnishing brush

Art carbon

Tracing paper

Stylus

Low tack tape

Retarder

Satin/gloss varnish

Colour palette

Russian Blue

Turquoise

Ocean Green

Cobalt Blue

Antique Gold

Hooker's Green

Yellow Oxide

Antique White

Burgundy

Purple Dioxide

Persian Rose

Terracotta

Burnt Umber

Ultramarine Blue

Yellow Light

Cadmium Yellow

INSTRUCTIONS

1 **Basecoat** Paint the entire tray with Russian Blue, using a 5 cm/2 in. sponge brush. When dry, make a loose marble mix of 2-parts Ocean Green to 1-part Cobalt Blue and 1-part Turquoise. Sponging into corners can be awkward so mask off the base and sides alternately. A deer foot stippler is used to stipple in the angle between the rim and the base. When dry, use your finger to rub Antique Gold along the edge and inside the handles.

2 Transfer the pattern.

3 **Rose leaves** Load the No. 3 round brush with a mid-green (Hooker's Green, Yellow Oxide and Antique White), and block in the leaves. Using the same green, side tip load with Antique White and follow the outer edges of the leaves with the wave stroke. Wipe off and flatten the brush on a tissue. With the semi-dry brush, pull the Antique White from the edges of the leaves down towards the centre. Tint the base and centre of the leaves with a wash of Hooker's Green. Use a No. 5/0 fine liner with the same wash to paint the veins.

4 **Tulip leaves** Load the No. 3 round brush with the mix of mid-green, side tip loaded with Hooker's Green on one side and Antique White on the other. Use flowing 'S' strokes.

5 **Small leaves** These are made up of little fat 'S' strokes using a No. 2 round brush, loaded with a very pale mix of green and side tip loaded with Antique White.

6 **Stems** Paint the stems with the No. 1 round brush loaded with a pale green watered down to an inky consistency.

7 Roses Basecoat each rose using a No. 3 round brush. The roses are different shades of pale Terracotta and pale Burgundy. When dry, use a No. 8 flat brush, side loaded in a deeper shade of their initial colour to shade the centre and base of each rose using a 'C' stroke. With a thin wash of Cadmium Yellow, tint the inside of the bowl of the roses. Working one rose at a time, apply a thin layer of retarder (see page 10). Load the No. 3 round brush with water and side tip load with Antique White. Starting with the back petals use 'C' strokes and the wave stroke to put in all the petals on the bowl of the rose. The outer petals are painted from the base upwards. Turn one or two petals over using the wave stroke.

8 Blue flowers Load the No. 3 round brush with Antique White, tip loaded with Ultramarine Blue. Paint in the back petals using the push/pull technique. Stipple the centre with Yellow Oxide, tip loaded with Antique White, and then add the front petals.

9 Yellow flowers Load the No. 2 round brush with Yellow Oxide, side loaded with Antique White. Each petal is made up from two facing comma strokes (with the side load of Antique White on the outside edges).

10 White flowers Finely stipple the centre of the flowers with a mid-green wash, using a marine sponge on a cocktail stick. Paint the petals with small comma strokes, using a No. 2 round brush loaded with Antique White. Stipple the centres with Yellow Light.

11 Tulips Load the No. 3 round brush with Antique White and block in both tulips. For the Burgundy tulip, reload with Antique White and side tip load with Burgundy. Use the wave stroke to outline the petal, wipe off excess on a tissue and pull a little colour in from the edges. Do not take the colour all the way to the base of the petal. When dry, make a very pale yellow mix of Yellow Light and Antique White. Turn the tulip upside-down, and tint the base by pulling the wash down from the base. Use the same method for the Persian Rose tulip but paint the base with Antique White. If the brush leaves a little puddle of paint when tinting, it is too wet. Simply rest the bristles on a tissue and start again. Stipple a little Yellow Oxide at the base of the stamens and paint in three stamens using Burnt Umber. Add the bases and stem using a No. 1 round brush loaded with pale green and side loaded with Hooker's Green.

12 Michelmas daisies Use a No. 1 round brush loaded with Purple Dioxide, wiped through a little Antique White. Paint the back row using little comma strokes. These petals must reach past the start of the stamens, so that they are tucked in behind them. Follow this by stippling the stamens of the flowers with the same brush loaded with Yellow Oxide and tip loaded with Antique White. Add the front rows of petals. The design template indicates single rows of petals, but add more as shown opposite on the worksheet.

13 Finishing Apply 2-3 coats of satin or gloss varnish.

Fruit basket on cabinet

This cabinet is painted in a monochrome, French Provincial style. The majority of the design is applied using a glaze of Indigo, side loaded and palette blended on to the flat brushes. Practise different elements of the pattern until you feel confident. This will also help you decide just how dark or light you would like the colour.

MATERIALS

Flat brushes
No. 6, 10, 18

Round brushes No. 2, 4

5 cm/2 in. sponge brush

Liner brush

Art carbon (blue)

Tracing paper

Low tack tape

Stylus

000 fine steel wool

Cling film

Cotton buds

Old toothbrush

Retarder

Antiquing medium

Satin varnish

Gloss varnish

Colour palette

Antique White

Indigo

Payne's Grey

Payne's Grey artists'
oil colour

INSTRUCTIONS

1 **Basecoat** Give the cabinet 2-3 coats of Antique White.

2 Transfer the fruit pattern on to the cabinet. This project uses thin washes of paint so a blue or water soluble art carbon should be used as the carbon lines may show beneath the glaze.

3 **Glaze** Mix some satin varnish or clear glazing medium with 2-3 drops retarder in a small dish. This medium will always be loaded on the brush before the Indigo is side loaded and blended. Because the mix has more body than water, it gives more control when using this technique on larger areas. Do not use white to reduce the shade as this will change the whole effect. Care must be taken not to overlap lines as all mistakes will show through the glaze. A damp cotton bud used quickly will mop up any overlaps. You may find it easier to use liquid masking to prevent the different elements from overlapping each other.

4 **Fruit leaves** These are painted using the ruffle technique. Both flat brushes are side loaded and palette blended with the Indigo glaze. Use the No. 18 flat brush for the grape leaves and the No. 6 flat brush for the apple leaves.

5 **Fruit** The No. 18 flat brush is used for the large pieces of fruit and the No. 10 flat brush is used for the grapes. With the brushes side loaded as required, use smooth sweeping strokes to outline the fruit with a soft blending of colour (see worksheet on page 94).

6 Stems Paint the stems with the No. 2 round brush loaded with the glaze mix and side tip loaded with Indigo.

7 Basket The coiled straw effect on the rim and base of the basket is made from a series of 'S' strokes using a No. 6 flat brush, side loaded with the Indigo glaze. Apply the criss-cross lines of the basket weave by keeping the dark edge of the side loaded brush pointing to the base of the basket. When dry, side load the No. 18 flat brush and shade the sides of the basket, as well as below the rim and base.

8 Butterfly and birds Side load the No. 6 flat brush and paint in the birds. Use the ruffle technique for the butterfly wings.

9 Leaves Load the No. 4 round brush with the Indigo glaze and paint the small sprays of leaves and those around the door using simple 'S' strokes.

10 Panels Side load the No. 18 flat brush with Indigo and paint the shading for the faux panels on the sides and door of the cabinet. To apply the straight lines on the side panel when there are no mouldings to follow, cut a 3 x 3 cm (1½ x 1½ in.) piece of straight timber to the length needed for your panels. Attach thick sticky felt pads on one side. This will hold it just above the surface to be painted, making it an excellent straight edge against which to rest the brush. If you have a steady hand, low tack tape is an alternative method.

11 Lightly fly speck the front and sides of the cabinet with a wash of Indigo (see page 15). Once this is dry, the lower part of the cabinet is ready to be distressed and antiqued. Rub the painting back with 000 fine steel wool and antique with Payne's Grey (see page 16).

12 Marble top The marbled effect on the top of the cabinet is created with a glaze of Payne's Grey and satin varnish with a few drops of retarder. Slosh this (yes, really!) over the surface, quickly lay a sheet of cling film and lift off straight away. This will leave a marbled effect. Study the design left by the cling film and use a damp cloth to lift out a few patches of the colour. Leave to dry. Add a little more Payne's Grey to the glaze and emphasize some of the lines using a liner brush (or goose feather), especially around the patches which have had the colour taken out.

13 Finishing When this is dry, apply several coats of gloss varnish.

Tip Low tack tape can be used to mitre the corners when running the shading down the edge of the panels.

Lace book box

The design on this book box was inspired as much by pictures of antique gold and silver filigree caskets as by antique pieces of lace which belonged to my mother. I find it fascinating to see how designs and artefacts reflect the period in which they were made. Although this design looks intricate, it consists mainly of comma strokes and just requires a little patience!

MATERIALS

Round brush No. 2

Flat brush No. 4

2 cm/¾ in. flat brush

Liner No. 5/0

Coarse household brush

30 cm/12 in. sponge brush

Soft make-up brush

Stylus

Tracing paper

Art carbon

Low tack tape

Antiquing medium

Satin varnish

Colour palette

Terracotta

Black

Antique White

Antique Gold

Burnt Umber

Burnt Umber artists' oil paint

4-parts satin varnish to 1-part Antique Gold with a dash of Burnt Umber. Working one side at a time, apply this mix and then quickly drag your coarse household brush across the surface, creating the impression of book leaves.

INSTRUCTIONS

1 **Basecoat** With a sponge brush paint the outside of the book box Black (the page leaves are Antique White) and the interior Terracotta.

2 **Pages** Paint the leaves of the book around the edge of the box in Antique White using the 2 cm/¾ in. flat brush. Then make up a mix of

3 Trace the design The design template which is a quarter section needs to be traced on each corner of the book box.

4 Lines Start by painting the lines with the 5/0 liner. Try to paint them all at the same sitting as you will build up a rhythm with the spacing.

5 Roses To paint in the roses use a No. 4 flat brush loaded with clear glazing medium or satin varnish, side loaded with Antique White. Use small commas for the petals and the wave stroke for the bowl of the rose.

6 Decide which of the motifs you will paint next and apply them with the No. 2 round brush. I find it useful to paint all the same elements in the design together and then move on to the next set.

7 Dots. All the dots are applied with the stylus. The graduated dots on the border are created by dipping your stylus into a pool of paint. Start at the top of the peak and without reloading, travel down the line (the dots will decrease in size as the paint runs out). If you need the dots to be uniform in size, renew the paint on the stylus every two dots.

8 Finishing Once dry, this can be antiqued with Burnt Umber or just varnished.

surface that it will not affect the acrylic paint used for painting the design.

5 Transfer the design. If you want it to look deeply crazed, add a little more crackle glaze to the tips of the scrolls and under the roses before you start to paint.

6 Scrolls Using a No. 6 round brush loaded with Yellow Oxide, paint the predominate part of the scroll by placing two comma strokes end to end. Add the fine lines and embellishments; accentuate with commas and 'S' strokes using Raw Sienna (see worksheet opposite).

7 Leaves Load a No. 4 or a No. 6 round brush with a mix of equal parts of Hooker's Green and Olive Green, plus enough satin varnish or clear glazing medium to make the mix translucent. Paint in the leaves, using simple comma and 'S' strokes.

8 Roses Give the roses a basecoat of the pale Persian Rose with the No. 4 round brush. Load the brush with pale rose pink then flatten and sideload with the dark Persian Rose (see page 26). Use the 'C' stroke with the darker shade pointing to the base of the rose, and shade the centre and base of the bowl. To paint the petals, load the brush with the pale mix of Persian Rose, then flatten and side load the brush with the dark Persian Rose (see page 26). Keeping the dark shade to the outer edges of the petals, define the back rows of petals using small comma strokes. Stipple the centres by loading the brush with orange made up of Yellow Oxide and Alizarin Crimson, kick loaded with Persian Rose. Use comma and wave strokes to define the outer petals and the bowl of the rose.

9 Erase all remaining tracing lines.

10 To give the wardrobe a soft, aged effect, mix the Titanium White artists' oil paint with the white spirit to a thin wash and wipe it over the whole surface of the wardrobe.

11 Finishing Do not brush a water-based varnish over the project. This will soften the crackle glaze and ruin your work. Only very thin oil-based washes are used over the crackle glaze to stain it. This will not be enough to provide a protective coat as in proper antiquing. Either use an acrylic spray varnish or an oil-based varnish to seal the surface.

Antique chest

This chest was also inspired by my visit to Russia. It is relatively simple as it uses very basic techniques, but you do need a little patience. I am very pleased with the effect and hope you enjoy this project. The design template has been coded with the first letter of the colours to be used. To make it easier to follow, you might like to put dots of the required colours over the letters, as this makes it much quicker for the eye to see when referring to the design.

MATERIALS

Round brushes No. 2, 4

Flat brush No. 8

Liner brush No. 5/0

5 cm/2 in. sponge brush

000 fine steel wool

Coarse household brush

Varnishing brush

Art carbon

Tracing paper

Stylus

Low tack tape

Antiquing medium

Satin varnish

Colour palette

Yellow Oxide

Antique White

Burnt Umber

Raw Umber

Terracotta

Hooker's Green

Indigo

Burnt Umber artists' oil paint

INSTRUCTIONS

1 **Background** Make up a pale yellow mix of Antique White and Yellow Oxide. When painting the background colour on the box you can use a coarse brush to create the ridged effect in wood. This is particularly effective on MDF or any other kind of fibreboard which has a very smooth surface. The ridges will be accentuated when you come to the final antiquing stage.

2 Transfer the design leaving out the fine detail.

3 Block in the Indigo panels and the Raw Umber cross bands with a No. 8 flat brush.

4 When this is dry, transfer the details on both the Yellow and Indigo panels.

5 **Horses** Paint the horses with a No. 4 round brush loaded with Raw Umber. Outline and detail with Burnt Umber using a No. 2 round brush.

6 All the small embellishments are painted alternately in Terracotta and Hooker's Green using the No. 4 round brush.

7 When all these details have been painted, outline everything with Burnt Umber using a No. 2 round brush or 5/0 liner. The outlines and dots on the Indigo panels are Yellow Oxide.

8 **Finishing** Use 000 steel wool to distress the chest around the corners and areas that would have taken the most wear and tear. Antique with Burnt Umber artists' oil paint and then satin varnish.

Design Templates

The 20 design templates illustrated in this section can be reduced or enlarged on a photocopier to the appropriate size to fit the piece you are painting. Once you have done this, trace the design straight on to the surface (see page 13).

BLUE AND WHITE TULIP TABLE

SUNFLOWER PLATTER

DAISY CHAIR

ROSE MAGAZINE RACK

COCKEREL PLAQUE

PANSY HAT BOX

POPPY BREAD BIN

LION BOOK BOX

SCROLL WASTEBIN

I INDIGO
O OLIVE GREEN
T TERRACOTTA

BLACKBERRY BREADBOARD

NAÏVE CLOCK

NAUTICAL LAP DESK

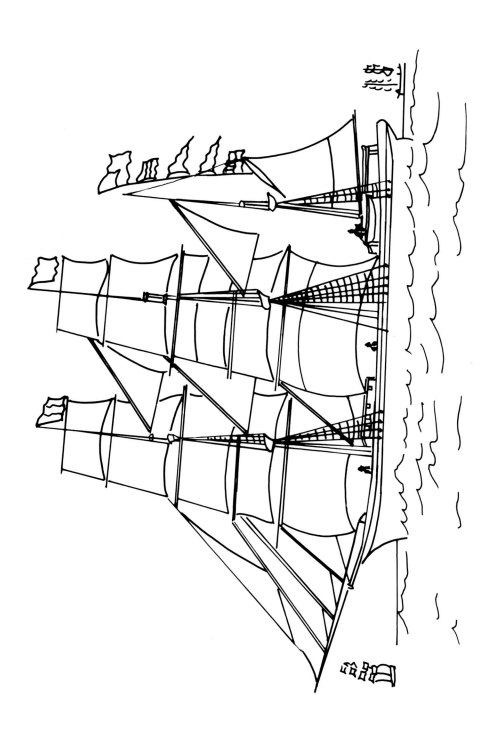

NAUTICAL LAP DESK

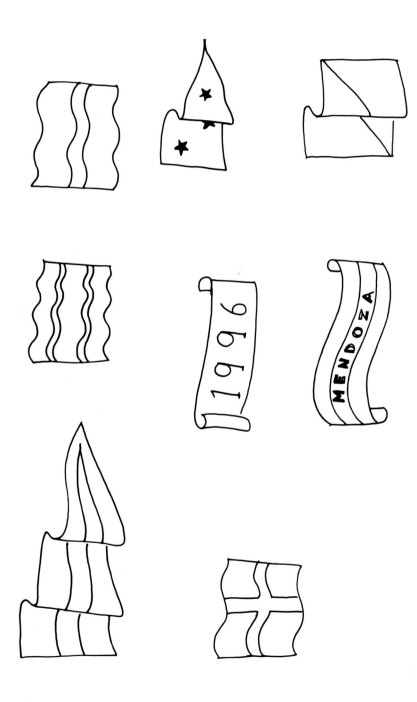

ROSE AND TULIP TRAY

FRUIT BASKET ON CABINET

FRUIT BASKET ON CABINET

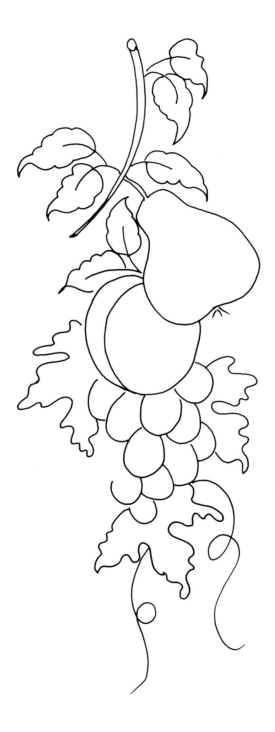

LACE BOOK BOX

FRENCH STYLE WARDROBE

ANTIQUE CHEST

ANTIQUE CHEST

o DOTS OF YELLOW OXIDE
T TERRACOTTA
I INDIGO
H HOOKER'S GREEN
R RAW UMBER
Y YELLOW OXIDE

BRUSHSTROKE PRACTISE SHEET

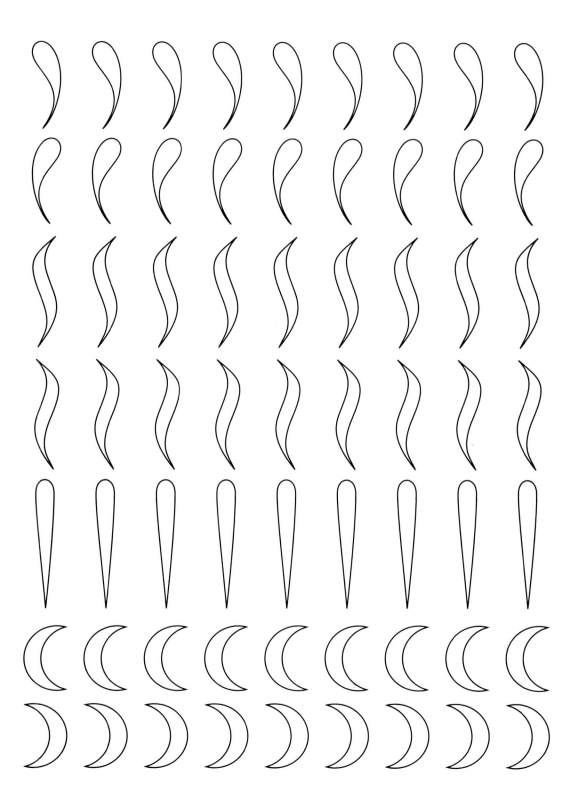

List of Suppliers

The Artist's Buying Club
13118 NE 4th Street
Vancouver, WA 98684
TEL 360-260-8877

Cabin Craft
1500 Westpark Way
Euless, TX 76040
TEL 817-571-3837
FAX 817-571-4925

Christopher S. Burch
216 W Hyde Park Place
Tampa, FL 33606
TEL 813-251-1522

CLC Designs Inc.
6204 Edith NE
Albuquerque, NM 87111
TEL 800-745-8707
FAX 505-344-4700

Covered Bridge Crafts
449 Amherst Street
Nashua, NH 03063
TEL 603-889-2179
FAX 603-882-5240

Decorative Artist's Workbook
1507 Dana Avenue
Cincinnati, OH 45207
TEL 800-283-0963

Decorative Artist's Book Club
1507 Dana Avenue
Cincinnati, OH 45207
TEL 513-531-8250

Gail's Brush & Palette
4159 S 76th Street
Milwaukee, WI 53220
TEL 414-321-6611

Grant Allison Decorative Painting Inc.
20 W 20th Street
New York, NY 10011
TEL 212-675-2286
FAX 212-675-2286

Homecraft Express Inc.
PO Box 24890
San Jose, CA 95154
TEL 800-301-7377
FAX 800-528-4193

The Paint Box
1540 NE 172nd Street
Portland, OR 97216
TEL 503-255-8560

Patty's Country Sampler
1931 N 3rd Street
Terre Haute, IN 47804
TEL 812-235-6896

Pitter Patter Pigtail Girls
2210 Silver Lane #308
Saint Paul, MN 55112
TEL 218-463-1984

Plain and Fancy
600 Baxter Lane
Nashville, TN 37220
TEL 615-373-3546
FAX 615-370-8503

Porcelain Tole Treasures
3446 McCutcheon Road
Columbus, OH 43230
TEL 614-471-7407

Priscilla's Little Red Tole House
PO Box 521013
Tulsa, OK 74152
TEL 918-743-6072
FAX 918-743-5075

Rococo Rose
3936 S Semoran Boulevard
Orlando, FL 32822
TEL 407-381-1142
FAX 407-380-9577

Sharon & Gayle Publications
601 Washington Avenue
Newport, KY 41071
TEL 606-655-4700
FAX 606-655-4702

Stan Brown Arts & Crafts
13435 NE Whitaker Way
Portland, OR 97230
TEL 503-257-0559

Steph's Folk Art Studio
2435 Old Philadelphia Park
Smoketown, PA 17576
TEL 717-299-4973

Stone Bridge Collection
RR 4
Parkenham, ON K0A 2X0
Canada
TEL 613-624-5080
FAX 613-624-5081

Teaberry Farms
1214 SE 159th Avenue
Vancouver, WA 98684
TEL 360-896-3571

Viking Woodcrafts Inc.
1317 8th Street SE
Waseca, MN 56093
TEL 507-835-8043
FAX 507-835-3895

Wet Paint Inc.
1684 Grand Avenue
Saint Paul, MN 55105
TEL 612-698-6431
FAX 612-698-8041

Woodworks
4521 Anderson Boulevard
Fort Worth, TX 76117
TEL 817-581-5230
FAX 817-581-5235

Index